Original title:
Frozen Tides

Author: Sebastian Sarapuu
ISBN HARDBACK: 978-9916-79-855-3
ISBN PAPERBACK: 978-9916-79-856-0
ISBN EBOOK: 978-9916-79-857-7

Enigma of the Frosted Abyss

In shadows deep, where whispers dwell,
The icy veil weaves secrets well.
Each crystal shard reflects the night,
In frozen depths, there stirs a light.

A dance of frost on silent breath,
An eternal hush, a dream of death.
Yet through the gloom, a flicker glows,
A tale of ages, softly flows.

Wreathed in Winter's Silver Cloak

Beneath the sky of ashen gray,
The world transformed, in fractals play.
Each branch adorned with snowy lace,
Nature's breath in slow embrace.

The ground, a canvas, pure and bright,
Beneath the moon's soft, silver light.
A tranquil peace, a whispered tune,
As shadows dance beneath the moon.

Tidal Dreams Encased in Ice

The ocean waves, now held in time,
A liquid song, now slow and mime.
Frozen dreams in azure beds,
Where ancient stories softly spread.

The echoes of the tempest's roar,
Trapped within the icy shore.
A silent world, where echoes cease,
And every breath brings quiet peace.

The Call of Ancient Waters

Beneath the surface, secrets weave,
In liquid depths where shadows grieve.
The pulse of ages calls to me,
An ancient song beneath the sea.

With each soft ripple, whispers rise,
Tales of longing, lost goodbyes.
In every wave, a story lies,
The call of depths, where silence cries.

A Stillness in Flow

In the gentle embrace of the night,
Rippling whispers dance under starlight.
Silence holds the secrets of dreams,
As time drifts slowly, or so it seems.

Stillness lingers in the soft glow,
Where shadows weave tales of long ago.
A moment captured, a breath held tight,
In the heart of the calm, pure delight.

Floating leaves upon the stream,
Each one tells a story, a fleeting dream.
Nature's symphony hums a tune,
Under the watchful gaze of the moon.

Beneath the surface, currents stir,
In muted tones, they softly confer.
Life flows quietly, unseen by most,
In tranquility's realm, we find our host.

As dawn draws near, colors ignite,
The orchestra swells, a pure delight.
In every ripple, life finds its way,
A stillness in flow, come what may.

Frigid Realms

In the breath of winter's chill,
Mountains rise, majestic and still.
Frosted whispers touch the trees,
Nature dons her icy degrees.

Silvery landscapes stretch for miles,
White blankets cover with gentle smiles.
Each flake falls with a tender grace,
Frigid realms hold their own embrace.

Frozen rivers hold secrets deep,
In dreams of warmth, the world does sleep.
Icicles glisten in the sunlight's kiss,
A world transformed, a frosty bliss.

Beneath the ice, life quietly stirs,
Hidden beneath, the heart concurs.
Even in cold, life’s pulse remains,
Frigid realms, yet warmth sustains.

As twilight falls, the stars appear,
A crystalline sky that feels so near.
In the quiet, peace unfurls,
In the magic of frigid worlds.

Echoing Crystals

In caverns dark, the echoes ring,
Crystals shimmer, a ghostly bling.
Each sound cascades off rock and stone,
In a symphony that feels alone.

Reflections dance on walls of light,
Breaking dawn through endless night.
Whispers of life in silence sway,
Echoing crystals guide the way.

Rays of color in every hue,
Tell of secrets held in the blue.
In the depths, where shadows creep,
You can find the dreams we keep.

Faint glimmers twinkle in the dark,
Beneath their shine lies a spark.
A world rebirthed in silence profound,
In echoed beauty, life is found.

Through winding paths, the journey glows,
Where reflections twist and softly flow.
In echoing chambers, souls entwine,
The essence of time, a sacred shrine.

Shrouded Waters

Beneath the veil of morning mist,
The waters hide, a gentle tryst.
Soft ripples whisper of untold fates,
A shrouded world that patiently waits.

In shadows deep, reflections fade,
Murmurs of secrets serenely played.
Each droplet carries a whispered song,
In the depths where we all belong.

Lily pads rest in quiet grace,
While fish glide softly, leaving no trace.
Silence reigns, a soothing balm,
Where chaos ceases, tranquility's calm.

Even the sun, shy and meek,
Dances lightly, a golden streak.
In the embrace of waters deep,
Lies a promise, a dream to keep.

As twilight creeps o'er the glassy sway,
Shrouded waters bid farewell to day.
In the quiet depths, stories unfold,
In whispers of life, bold yet untold.

Distant Glows

In the night sky, stars appear,
Whispers of light, far and near.
Moonlit dreams in shadows dance,
Twinkling gems, a fleeting chance.

Waves of warmth on cold, dark shores,
Echoes of hope that time restores.
Guiding hearts through endless night,
Distant glows, a beacon bright.

Each flicker tells a story bold,
Of love long lost and tales retold.
In silent skies, their secrets flow,
Painting paths where wanderers go.

Yearning souls beneath the vast,
Chasing shadows of the past.
In quiet moments, time stands still,
Distant glows ignite the will.

So as the world slips into dreams,
The universe whispers gentle themes.
Under starlit blankets, we roam,
Distant glows call us home.

The Weight of Chill

Beneath the sky of leaden gray,
Winter sighs, as cold holds sway.
Frosty breath on windowpanes,
Nature sleeps, in icy chains.

Shadows stretch, the daylight wanes,
A shiver runs through empty lanes.
Silent trees with branches bare,
Whisper softly, an empty prayer.

Footsteps crunch on frozen ground,
Echoes linger, without sound.
Frigid winds through alleyways,
A testament to winter's ways.

In the still, the heartache stirs,
Memories lost, the warmth prefers.
The weight of chill wraps tight and close,
Yet spring remains a whispered hope.

So bear the cold, embrace the night,
For every shadow hides a light.
In the silence, find the thrill,
Within the weight of winter's chill.

Remnants of Surrender

Leaves that fall without a fight,
Whirl and twirl in fading light.
Whispers haunt the quiet ground,
Where lost dreams and hope abound.

In the stillness, echoes fade,
Of battles fought and debts unpaid.
A quiet heart begins to rest,
Finding peace, it feels the best.

Time's embrace, a gentle hold,
Warming paths once icy cold.
Every scar tells tales of grace,
Remnants left in life's embrace.

As dusk descends, the world gives in,
To soft shadows where love begins.
In surrender, we find our song,
In the quiet, we are strong.

With every breath, let go of pain,
In the remnants, we remain.
Finding strength in letting be,
In surrender, we are free.

The Arctic's Lament

Icebergs drift in silent woe,
Cries of nature swept below.
Frozen tears upon the seas,
The Arctic whispers soft pleas.

Winds lament the seals’ lost cries,
Echoes of life beneath the skies.
Each storm bears witness to the plight,
Of fragile worlds fading from sight.

Glistening shores, a beauty rare,
Hide the burdens that they bear.
As glaciers weep, the oceans rise,
A somber truth beneath bright skies.

In the dance of frost and fire,
The heart of nature's strong desire.
To mend the cloth of all that's torn,
To rally hope beneath the storm.

So heed the cries, the Arctic calls,
For in the silence, nature falls.
In every whisper, every breath,
We bear the call beyond the death.

The Breath of Winter

The chill whispers softly,
Through the branches so bare.
Snowflakes dance gently,
In the crisp, frosty air.

Frozen rivers are still,
Under blankets of white.
The moon glows with a thrill,
In the heart of the night.

Each breath forms a cloud,
As the world holds its peace.
Wrapped in silence loud,
Nature's sweet release.

Frost clings to the pines,
A shimmering dress worn.
Time gently aligns,
A new day is born.

Beneath the bright stars,
The earth is aglow.
In winter's deep bars,
Our spirits will grow.

In the Arms of Ice

Wrapped in winter's embrace,
Under blankets of frost.
The world slows its pace,
A beauty that's lost.

Icicles hang like tears,
From the edge of the eaves.
Whispering through the years,
Nature quietly grieves.

Amidst barren trees,
The stillness is profound.
Crisp air cuts with ease,
As silence wraps around.

The echo of the cold,
Calls out across the land.
A story left untold,
In winter's gentle hand.

Beneath azure skies,
The world holds its breath tight.
In the arms of ice,
We find warmth in the night.

Embraced by Stillness

In a realm so hushed,
Where the snowflakes lay thick,
Each moment is crushed,
With time's gentle tick.

The silence whispers sweet,
While shadows take their flight.
A stillness so complete,
In the arms of the night.

Footsteps fade away,
On the paths made of dreams.
As the cold starts to sway,
With its icy cold beams.

Every breath is a sigh,
A moment held in peace.
As the days drift by,
And the noise finds its cease.

Bound by winter's grace,
We linger, soft and slow.
In this tranquil place,
Where the wild winds don't blow.

Lament of the Unfrozen

The earth weeps in white,
For the warmth left behind.
Frigid winds take flight,
In the cold, they unwind.

Echoes of the past,
Linger within the chill.
A shadow that is cast,
By a warmth that is still.

Branches reach for the sky,
But the leaves have all fled.
With a longing sigh,
For the life that is dead.

Frostbitten whispers call,
Through the valleys so gray.
A soft, haunting thrall,
Of the warmth’s slow decay.

In the still of the night,
We remember the sun.
But winter holds tight,
To the chains it has spun.

The Undoing of Warmth

A flicker dims in shadowed light,
The golden rays begin to wane.
Once vibrant whispers, now take flight,
The chill arrives, a gentle bane.

In silent dusk, the world turns cold,
As laughter fades with autumn's breath.
Embrace of winter’s arms unfold,
A dance of stillness, whispering death.

The gentle fire struggles to hold,
Each flickering ember fights for breath.
Yet warmth in hearts can still be bold,
To ward off frost, to conquer death.

From ashes rise a muted glow,
A soft persistence, faint yet bright.
In unity, we learn to grow,
And face the long and lonely night.

So even as the warmth may flee,
Together, we resist the chill.
In bonds of love, we find the key,
A flame that flickers, strong and still.

Mysteries of the North

In shadows cast by towering pines,
The whispers of the ancients keep.
Through shivering winds, the truth entwines,
Awakening secrets buried deep.

The northern lights weave tales of old,
In colors swirling, vibrant, bold.
They beckon forth the daring souls,
To seek the treasure in the cold.

Thick blankets of snow hide what's near,
The stories lost beneath the frost.
But heart and spirit, fueled by fear,
Will journey forth, though paths are crossed.

The rivers flow with wisdom past,
Their currents guide the brave to roam.
In every glance, a spell is cast,
The North reveals its quiet home.

So venture forth with open eyes,
In every shadow, find the light.
In icy realms where mystery lies,
The North shall wrap you in its night.

Nature's Still Heart

In tranquil woods where silence dwells,
The heart of nature beats so softly.
Among the trees, a magic spells,
In whispers that flow, pure and lofty.

The gentle streams in peaceful flow,
Reflecting sunbeams, pure and bright.
Each rustle hints at stories low,
Where shadows dance with soft moonlight.

A mountain stands with silent grace,
Its rugged form a guardian true.
With every breeze, the wild embrace,
Reminds us of what’s great and new.

In fields where wildflowers bloom,
A canvas painted fresh and free.
Each petal holds the sun's own loom,
Weaving colors harmoniously.

So pause awhile and feel the calm,
Let nature cradle you in peace.
Her still heart offers gentle balm,
A refuge where our worries cease.

Serene Desolation

A barren land, so stark and grand,
Yet beauty twinkles in the gloom.
The quiet speaks, a soft demand,
To find the life in every tomb.

Amidst the ruins, memories breathe,
Each stone a story, rich and deep.
In silence, we begin to weave,
The tapestry of those who sleep.

The sunset paints the sky in dreams,
For every ending holds a spark.
In desolation, hope still gleams,
A light that flickers in the dark.

From ashes rise the seeds of grace,
Resilience thriving through the pain.
In solitude, we find a space,
To honor loss, to stand again.

So let us stand on sacred ground,
Embrace the empty, hear the call.
In serene desolation found,
We learn to rise from every fall.

Icy Currents of Time

The river flows with heavy sighs,
A chill that steals the warmth of day.
It whispers tales of groundless skies,
Where fleeting moments drift away.

Each flake of snow, a memory,
Caught in the grasp of autumn's breath.
A dance of frost, a cold decree,
That hints at life, yet shadows death.

Time shimmers like the frozen lake,
Beneath its surface, stories lie.
The current moves, a soft intake,
And carries dreams that never die.

In depths of blue, the secrets wear,
An icy veil, a timeless game.
As moments freeze, we stand and stare,
At echoes lost to frozen flame.

Chilled Whisper of the Waves

The ocean murmurs soft and low,
A tranquil breath on the white sand.
It weaves through dusk, a whisper’s flow,
As twilight paints the sea so grand.

Each crest of foam, a gentle sigh,
Leaves ripples dancing on the shore.
With every kiss of the night sky,
The waves reveal their ancient lore.

They tell of journeys far and wide,
Of storms and calm, of fierce embrace.
In shadows deep, they're hard to bide,
Yet in their depths, there’s quiet grace.

The breeze exhales a cool caress,
And salty air renews the soul.
In every wave, a soft recess,
Where memories swirl and dreams unroll.

Shards of Crystal Dreams

In crystal light, the visions gleam,
Fragile fragments of what could be.
They shimmer bright, a fleeting dream,
Reflecting hopes, but hard to see.

Each broken piece, a story told,
Of love and loss, of joy and pain.
They catch the light, their beauty bold,
Yet whisper softly, loss's gain.

The dreams we weave in silent night,
Like shards of glass, can cut so deep.
Yet in their brokenness, there's light,
A truth to hold and gently keep.

In each facet, a new chance lies,
To mend the heart and find our way.
The shards will guide beneath the skies,
Where dawn will turn to pitch-dark gray.

Frigid Embrace of the Sea

The sea reveals its coldest face,
A steel-blue expanse beneath the stars.
It beckons forth with silent grace,
And carries dreams, like wandering cars.

In depths where shadows linger long,
The frigid touch soaks through the bone.
Yet within the depths, there's a song,
A haunting call, forever known.

The waves caress with icy hands,
A chilling grip that holds so tight.
Yet all around, life understands,
That even cold can birth the light.

In every swell, the pulse of fate,
The tide that rises, falls away.
The sea embraces each heartbeat's state,
In its frigid hold, we learn to sway.

Shifting Glistens

In morning light they dance and play,
A shimmer here, then swept away.
Like whispers soft from skies above,
Each glisten tells a tale of love.

With every turn the colors shift,
In gentle winds, they rise and lift.
A fleeting breath, a moment's grace,
Nature's art in time and space.

Beneath the sun, they twinkle bright,
A kaleidoscope, pure delight.
They weave through dreams like silver threads,
Awakening the heart that treads.

As daylight fades, they start to wane,
Yet still they leave their glistening stain.
In twilight's arms, they softly gleam,
A quiet hush, a whispered dream.

Chilled Longing

Through frosted panes, the world feels far,
A silent void, where shadows are.
Each breath a cloud, as echoes ring,
Chilled longing sings of winter’s sting.

In corners dark, the memories freeze,
The warmth of touch, a distant tease.
I reach for dreams that slip away,
In twilight's grasp, I yearn and sway.

A fragile heart, encased in ice,
Yearning for love, a high-priced vice.
With every glimmer, hope ignites,
In the depth of night, my heart still fights.

The snowflakes drift, like time they fall,
In chilly whispers, I hear their call.
They find their place, a soft embrace,
And warm the chill with gentle grace.

Captive in Ice

Bound by frosty chains that gleam,
In the heart of winter's dream.
Thoughts encased in crystal's sheen,
Captive in ice, where none have been.

Silence wraps like a velvet cloak,
A frozen world where whispers choke.
Each shadow dances, a ghostly spire,
The quiet fuels a hidden fire.

In solitude, the heart will thaw,
While icy bars still hold in awe.
Yet hope awakes at dawn's first light,
The chains will break, and take to flight.

Beneath the frost, seeds start to grow,
Emerging where the winds won't blow.
As warmth returns, the spirit soars,
No longer trapped behind closed doors.

Subtle Crystals

A glimmer on the edge of night,
Subtle crystals, a charming sight.
They catch the moon in shards so clear,
Reflecting dreams of those held dear.

With each soft turn, they shift and sway,
In twilight's breath, they drift away.
A dance of light, a fleeting game,
Inscribed in air, but not the same.

Each delicate form, a story spun,
Of love and loss, of battles won.
Whispers echo in the dark,
Subtle crystals leave their mark.

In quiet rooms, they softly gleam,
A world of wonders, a gilded dream.
Where hearts collide and dance with fate,
In subtle shadows, love awaits.

The Beauty of Hibernation

In silent woods, the whispering trees,
Embrace the stillness of winter's freeze.
A blanket of white, serene and deep,
Nature rests now, in tranquil sleep.

The world slows down, time takes its pause,
Bathed in silence, without a cause.
Creatures nestle, snug and warm,
Wrapped in the peace that comes from the storm.

Stars twinkle bright in the frosty air,
Each sparkle dances, without a care.
Moonlight reflects on the glistening snow,
A beauty that's calm, a soft, gentle glow.

Days are shorter, nights stretch long,
In this quiet, we find our song.
With every breath, a crystal sigh,
In hibernation, we learn to fly.

So let us cherish this season's grace,
In the heart of winter, find our place.
For in the stillness, we will find,
The beauty of hibernation, redefined.

Isolation's Caress

In the silence of a shadowed room,
Isolation wraps like a billowing plume.
Walls close in, yet thoughts take flight,
Searching for warmth in the depth of night.

The clock ticks slow, each second drawn,
A dance with solitude, dusk till dawn.
Echoes of laughter remain unheard,
In the hush, my heart feels stirred.

Windows frame the world outside,
Life goes on, while I abide.
A solitary candle flickers near,
Its soft glow hushes every fear.

Yet in these moments, deep and bare,
I learn to weave with gentle care.
Threads of solitude, stitched with grace,
In isolation's caress, I find my space.

For sometimes silence speaks the truth,
Whispers of wisdom from the fountain of youth.
In solitude's arms, I grow and achieve,
Finding solace in the art of breathe.

Cascades of Frost

Morning light with a shimmer, a glow,
Cascades of frost, artfully flow.
Nature's canvas dressed in fine lace,
Every crystal sparkling in place.

Branches adorned with delicate crowns,
The earth wears a shroud, pure and brown.
Footsteps crunch on the frozen ground,
In this beauty, the world is found.

Soft whispers of chill in the air,
Nature's breath sings a song so rare.
A moment to pause, to take it all in,
As cascades of frost invite us to spin.

From the rooftops, the icicles hang,
In harmony with the frostbite’s tang.
Like jewels they shimmer in sunlight's embrace,
Cascades of frost, a moment of grace.

So let us rejoice in winter's art,
In every flake, warms the heart.
For in each cascade, we see the divine,
A fleeting beauty, forever enshrined.

A Dance of Shadows

When twilight falls, shadows take flight,
They waltz across the canvas of night.
In the flicker of lanterns, they sway,
A mystic dance, leading the way.

Softly they whisper, secrets so sweet,
A harmony born where dark and light meet.
Figures entwined in a delicate play,
A dance of shadows, come what may.

The moon casts a glow on the silent ground,
In this embrace, tranquility found.
Each shade a story, each form a tale,
Where heartbeats echo and dreams prevail.

As midnight drapes her velvet cloak,
Around the world, a soft-spoken yoke.
In this realm where whispers collide,
A dance of shadows, we gracefully glide.

So let the night, with its magic, unfurl,
In the rhythm of darkness, let spirits whirl.
For in shadows, we find our release,
A dance of pure, unspoken peace.

Moonlit Slumber of Submerged Sands

Beneath the waves, the night does gleam,
In silver light, where shadows dream.
Coral blooms in soft embrace,
As tides of time, the starlight chase.

Whispers of the ocean's song,
Echoes where the lost belong.
The moonlight kisses every shell,
In tranquil depths, where secrets dwell.

Crabs scuttle in a moonlit trance,
While fish in silken silvers dance.
Soft currents wrap their cool caress,
In the serenity, we find solace.

The sands lay still, so calm and pure,
Each grain a gem, the heart's allure.
In night’s sweet arms, we drift away,
To slumber ‘neath the waves’ soft play.

Together with the tide we float,
On dreams that whisper, gently quote.
In moonlit slumber, life expands,
In harmony with submerged sands.

Glinting Armor of the Briny Deep

From depths below, the treasures gleam,
In glinting light, like fractured dreams.
The armor shines with tales untold,
In shades of silver, blue, and gold.

Creatures swim in hazy light,
Guardians of the darkened night.
Each scale a piece of history,
In the briny depths, wild and free.

With every wave, a story swells,
Where echoes of the ocean dwells.
The spark of life, profound and grand,
In shining forms, we take our stand.

Glistening shells and tangled weeds,
Nature's bounty fulfills our needs.
Through realms of shadow, we will creep,
Beneath the glinting armor, deep.

Together bound by sea and time,
In salty waves, we find our rhyme.
The briny deep, a timeless sweep,
A treasure trove, where secrets keep.

Twilight Dance on Snow-Capped Shores

The twilight casts a golden hue,
On snow-capped shores where time is new.
Footprints fade in the frosty sand,
As nature waves its gentle hand.

The ocean murmurs soft and sweet,
In harmony, the waves retreat.
A dance of light and shadow plays,
As dusk unfolds its velvet gaze.

Seagulls cry in the cooling air,
A celebration, wild and rare.
The sunset paints the sky with fire,
As day gives way to night's desire.

Waves whisper secrets to the night,
In soft embrace of fading light.
The world transforms, a sight to keep,
In twilight's dance, the spirits leap.

Together we will watch and dream,
As twilight bathes the shores in cream.
In this embrace, our hearts explore,
The magic found on winter's shore.

The Veil of the Winter Sea

A whisper flows through chilly air,
As winter wraps the sea with care.
The waves wear coats of frosted lace,
A delicate and tranquil grace.

The horizon blushes with soft hue,
While fog descends, a dream anew.
In silent swirls, the ocean sighs,
Beneath the gaze of leaden skies.

Each wave a story, slow and wise,
In silvered foam where magic lies.
The sea snakes glide through misty veils,
In winter's grasp, where silence dwells.

The world stands still, a breath held tight,
While stars peek through the cloak of night.
In icy grip, the sea does gleam,
A haunting whisper, a forgotten dream.

Together we will brave the chill,
Embrace the quiet, time will still.
In the veiled embrace of winter's sea,
We find our hearts forever free.

Lament of the Frosty Horizon

The sky weeps tears of ice,
As daylight flees from night.
Silent winds begin to slice,
Whispering a cold delight.

Barren trees in frozen grace,
Stand like ghosts in pale array.
Nature dons a stark embrace,
As shadows dance and sway.

Rippling rivers, frozen wide,
Beneath a shroud of crystal air.
Echoes of the winter tide,
Linger softly everywhere.

In the distance, mountains frown,
Their peaks adorned with silver light.
The sun dips low, and twilight's gown
Enfolds the world in quiet night.

A lament for warmth and bloom,
In every heart, a flicker fades.
Yet in this frigid, solemn gloom,
The beauty flows, and hope cascades.

The Crystalline Chorus of the Deep

In the depths, silence reigns,
Where shadows weave and swirl.
Shimmering whispers, lost refrains,
In the ocean's secret whirl.

Softly swaying, kelp entwined,
Underneath the weight of dreams.
Every current, gently lined,
With the echoes of moonbeams.

Glow of phosphorescent light,
Guides the way through darkened seas.
Melodies of day and night,
Carried softly on the breeze.

Creatures dance in liquid gold,
In this realm of nature's art.
Stories of the brave and bold,
Written in the sailor's heart.

Yet the beauty hides its face,
Secret passages remain unclear.
Each wave sings with timeless grace,
In the depths, where few will steer.

Chilling Shadows on the Surf

Upon the shore, the shadows creep,
Cast by twilight's gentle hand.
Waves that whisper, lull and leap,
Dance along the silver sand.

Frosty mists embrace the night,
As moonlight weaves a ghostly path.
Softly glimmering, a fleeting sight,
Lingers in the aftermath.

Seagulls cry, a haunting call,
Echoes blend with ocean's sigh.
Nighttime's veil enshrouds all,
Underneath the starry sky.

Footprints left where dreams reside,
Trace the edges of the vast.
In this realm, our thoughts confide,
Memories of shades cast fast.

Yet each wave that comes to shore,
Brings a tale of times gone by.
Chilling shadows, evermore,
Bound to dance with the tide's sigh.

The Frosted Dew of Distant Shores

Morning breaks with icy breath,
Upon the sands of time's embrace.
Silent whispers greet the death,
Of night, in frost's soft lace.

Dew drops shimmer in the light,
Like diamonds graced by morning's glow.
Each droplet holds a fleeting sight,
Of dreams we yearn, of tales we know.

Waves that lap with tender grace,
Kiss the earth with a gentle sigh.
In the quiet, find your place,
As morning glories rise and fly.

Breezes carry stories old,
From lands afar, where rivers flow.
In their whispers, truth is told,
Of journeys past, in twilight's show.

Yet in this frosted morning light,
Hope unfurls its tender wings.
Embrace the day, fresh and bright,
As the world with love now sings.

Frostbitten Remnants of Forgotten Shores

The waves once kissed the silent sand,
Leaves of ice now grasp the land.
Footprints etched in frozen clasp,
Echoes whisper, time's firm grasp.

Shells encased in crystalline glow,
Memories of warmth, long gone, slow.
The horizon blurs in twilight's breath,
A dance of frost, a tale of death.

Silent shadows drift and sway,
Tales of sailors lost at bay.
Beneath the chill, their voices hum,
Lost to time, forever numb.

In the stillness, secrets keep,
Buried deep, where waters weep.
Glimmers fade in the moon's soft light,
Frostbitten dreams, lost to night.

The ocean's song, a haunting plea,
To the shores of lost memory.
Frostbitten remnants, windswept shore,
A tale of love, forever more.

The Melting Secrets of North Winds

Whispers ride the frozen air,
Stories loom, hidden with care.
The north winds breathe, a chilling song,
Tales of journeys, where hearts belong.

Melting edges of fate collide,
Fragments where the secrets bide.
Underneath the snowy veil,
Ancient voices tell their tale.

Invisible threads in the twilight dance,
A cadence of dreams, a fleeting chance.
The crisp air trembles, secrets weave,
In the night, what we believe.

Upon the glacier, stories we trace,
Echoes of a forgotten place.
With each gust, memories stir,
In the silence, feelings blur.

The melting secrets, delicate chart,
Reveal the paths of the wandering heart.
In nature's fold, we find the key,
To the whispers of eternity.

Abyss of Rime and Silence

Deep in the void, where shadows creep,
Rime blankets all in a shroud of sleep.
Silence reigns in the frozen deep,
With secrets of lost souls to keep.

Glacial echoes float in the air,
Stories woven from despair.
In the abyss, time stands still,
Emotions freeze, against our will.

Beneath the frost, a world concealed,
Wonders lost, fate unsealed.
Each flake whispers, a vision shared,
A canvas of dreams, beautifully bared.

In the shadows, what lies beneath?
A dance of silence, a tangled wreath.
The rime portrays, with gentle sigh,
Life's fragile thread beneath the sky.

Here in the void, we bare our souls,
Seeking warmth as rime extols.
In the abyss, where stillness reigns,
A longing heart, forever wanes.

Snowbound Whispers of the Ocean

Frosty waves, on shores they break,
In silence stitched, the heavens quake.
Snowbound whispers, secrets flow,
The ocean hides, what few may know.

Against the tide, the chill imparts,
Rippling echoes of gentle hearts.
From deep within, a mournful tune,
Songs of longing, 'neath the moon.

Frozen dreams, encased in blue,
Carried far, like morning dew.
With every wave, a sigh is caught,
In the chill, emotions taught.

In the depths, where shadows play,
The ocean's breath leads hearts astray.
Snowbound whispers linger long,
In the stillness, a timeless song.

As the horizon swallows light,
Hope remains, in the frozen night.
Beneath the snow, the ocean's heart,
Awaits the spring, to once depart.

Tranquil Shadows

In the whisper of dusk, shadows play,
Silhouettes dance where the light fades away.
Gentle breezes weave through the trees,
Carrying secrets on a soft, cool breeze.

Moonlight drapes softly, a silvery sheet,
Nature's calm heartbeat, a soothing repeat.
Stars peek through the veil of the night,
Guiding lost souls with their tender light.

Reflections in lakes, a quiet embrace,
Mirrored thoughts in this tranquil space.
Here, time stands still, and worries cease,
In the realm of shadows, I find my peace.

Beneath the vast sky, all burdens dissolve,
In the art of stillness, the heart can evolve.
Here, every moment feels like a dream,
Flowing gently like a soft, crystal stream.

Iced Horizons

On the edge of the world, where cold winds blow,
Iced horizons stretch, in a pure, white glow.
Frosted whispers kiss the winters deep,
In silence, the earth sings a song to keep.

Glistening crystals catch the morning light,
Nature's adornments, a breathtaking sight.
Footsteps crunch softly over snow-laden ground,
In this frozen wilderness, peace can be found.

Pines stand tall, draped in winter's embrace,
Guardians of secrets, holding their grace.
Beyond the horizon, beauty untamed,
In the heart of the cold, our souls are reclaimed.

A world painted white, serene and grand,
In the stillness we find, the warmth of the land.
Every flake a promise, unique in its make,
In this icy expanse, we nurture and wake.

Crystalized Dreams

In the dawn's early light, dreams take flight,
Crystalized visions shimmer, pure and bright.
Each thought a reflection, delicate and rare,
Floating softly on the edges of air.

Morning dew clings to petals of grace,
Nature's own jewels in this sacred place.
With every heartbeat, the dreams intertwine,
Crafting a tapestry, wondrous design.

In the quiet of night, when the world is still,
Dreams dance like shadows upon the hill.
Whispers of magic softly unfold,
In the embrace of the night, secrets told.

Through the lens of the heart, we seek to explore,
Every crystalized dream, an open door.
With courage, we journey, hand in hand,
Into realms unknown, together we stand.

Glistening Quiet

In the still of the morn, the world holds its breath,
Glistening quiet, a moment of depth.
Sunbeams break gently through the soft haze,
Illuminating paths in a warm, golden blaze.

Fields stretch in silence, bathed in soft light,
Whispers of nature take gentle flight.
Birds sing the dawn, a melodious cheer,
In this glistening quiet, all things feel near.

Every leaf glimmers, a story untold,
Nature’s reflection in hues radiant and bold.
With each heartbeat, a promise alive,
In the calm of this moment, our spirits thrive.

Beneath the vast sky, hope finds its voice,
In the glistening quiet, we rejoice.
With open hearts, we embrace the day,
In the dance of the light, we find our way.

Silent Depths of Winter's Gaze

In the hush of falling snow,
Whispers from the frozen ground,
Dreams of warmth and sunlight glow,
Amidst the silence, peace is found.

Trees stand still, their branches bare,
Blankets white on nature's bed,
Cold winds weave a tranquil air,
In winter's heart, the world lies dead.

Stars above in crystal night,
Glimmer through the frosty haze,
Each breath fogs, a fleeting sight,
In silent depths of winter's gaze.

Time slows down, a gentle pause,
As nature holds its breath in grace,
Softly feels the chill’s warm claws,
Embracing all with frozen lace.

Life will wake with colors bright,
As seasons turn and days grow long,
But in this deep, Ah! Such delight,
In winter's song, I feel belong.

Glacial Echoes of Distant Shores

Upon the coast where icebergs play,
Whispers ride the ocean's breath,
Glacial echoes softly sway,
A haunting sound of beauty's death.

Frozen waves kiss rocky strands,
Where time stands still, the earth holds tight,
In every crest, a painter's hands,
Craft scenes of stillness wrapped in white.

Mist hangs low, a ghostly shroud,
Clouds gather close, a muted sky,
With every wave, the sea is loud,
Yet quietude beneath the cry.

Salt and ice create a song,
That only those who listen know,
In glacial depths, the heart beats strong,
Where distant shores hold stories slow.

Nature's choir sings from afar,
Each note a testament to time,
In frozen realms, we find the star,
That guides us through the winter's chime.

The Stillness Beneath the Ice

In tranquil pools of crystal clear,
Where time rests in a frozen state,
Secrets whisper, calm and near,
The stillness holds a quiet fate.

Beneath the surface lies a world,
Of life embraced in chilly grip,
As snowflakes dance and softly swirled,
In dreams of warmth that softly slip.

Branches arch like fingers wise,
Reaching down to touch the lake,
Mirrored sky in winter’s guise,
Reflecting all the dreams we make.

Silence sings a frosty tune,
While shadows cast in silver light,
Nature's cloak, a softened rune,
In stillness deep, we find our sight.

Awaiting spring's soft, gentle kiss,
Beneath the ice, a heart does stir,
Each moment holds a precious bliss,
In winter's grasp, the pulse is sure.

Shimmering Veil of Winter's Breath

A quilt of frost on window panes,
Breathing patterns soft and light,
Winter paints with icy veins,
Dancing shadows of the night.

Underneath a shimmering veil,
The world transformed in crystal sheen,
Each step echoes in the pale,
As silence falls, the landscape’s clean.

Light cascades through frosty air,
Glittering jewels on trees so grand,
Footprints mark the pathway's care,
In winter's breath, we understand.

Moments held in frozen time,
The heartbeat of a world asleep,
Within the chill, a quiet rhyme,
Of nature's charm, so vast and deep.

When spring arrives to kiss the earth,
And melt away the winter's woe,
We'll hold the magic of its birth,
In shimmering tales of ice and snow.

Frigid Harmony

In the silence of winter's embrace,
Snowflakes whisper without a trace.
Branches bow with the weight they bear,
Nature sleeps in the crisp, cold air.

Moonlight dances on frozen streams,
Casting shadows, weaving dreams.
The world holds its breath, stark and bright,
As stars twinkle in the quiet night.

Footsteps crunch on the powdery ground,
A symphony heard all around.
Each breath mingles with frosty air,
In frigid harmony, no need to care.

Trees stand tall, dressed in white,
Guardians of the tranquil night.
Their secrets wrapped in a timeless shroud,
Whispering truths soft, yet loud.

As dawn breaks, the colors ignite,
Painting the world with warmth and light.
A fleeting moment, then winter calls,
In frigid harmony, beauty enthralls.

Reflections on Cold Waters

Beneath the ice, the river flows,
Whispers of life that few truly know.
Ripples shimmer in muted grace,
Mirroring clouds in a silvered face.

Frost-kissed banks where shadows play,
Fleeting glimpses of a brighter day.
Each drop a story, each wave a song,
In cold waters, where dreams belong.

Silence reigns, save the soft sigh,
Of nature resting beneath the sky.
Fragments of light, like promises shared,
Reflecting the hopes that once were declared.

In winter's grasp, the world feels still,
Yet waters pulse with unspoken thrill.
The beauty lies in what's beneath,
Where life stirs slowly, unseen wreath.

And as the thaw begins its dance,
Life reawakens, takes its chance.
Rippling laughter, a joyous spree,
Reflections sparkle, wild and free.

The Larval Depth

Deep in the shadows where secrets dwell,
Life stirs in silence, a hidden spell.
Larvae thrive in the murky gloom,
Awaiting the light to break through the tomb.

Gentle currents cradle their dreams,
Among the weeds, where darkness teems.
Each movement hints at futures bright,
In the larval depth, concealed from sight.

Nature's patience, a timeless grace,
As each tiny creature finds its place.
A journey starts in the darkest night,
Transcending shadows, seeking the light.

Emergence beckons, a call so clear,
From the depths, they shed their fear.
Metamorphosis whispers in the air,
A promise of wings, a life to share.

In the larval depth, beginnings bloom,
Transforming stillness into vibrant plume.
Life's cycle spins in unseen art,
From darkest waters to a soaring heart.

Crystalline Veils

In the morning light, the frost appears,
Draped like jewels, shimmering spheres.
Crystalline veils adorn each tree,
Nature's tapestry, wild and free.

Each breath released in the frosty air,
Transforms to diamonds, vibrant and rare.
Sunrise kisses the icy threads,
Awakening color where stillness spreads.

Hidden wonders in icy embrace,
Whispering stories of time and space.
Delicate patterns, intricate designs,
Nature's artistry, where beauty shines.

With every gust, the veils will sway,
A fleeting dance before they fray.
But magic lingers in the chill,
Crystalline veils evoke a thrill.

As winter wanes, they gently fade,
Yet memories linger, never betrayed.
In echoes of ice, a soft farewell,
Life's transient art, a crystalline spell.

Beneath the Surface

In quiet depths where shadows play,
Secrets linger, lost in gray.
Whispers soft, the echoes urge,
A world concealed, a silent surge.

Coral dreams on sapphire beds,
Tales of old that darkness spreads.
Fins that dance with muted grace,
Life beneath in a hidden space.

Currents pull with gentle might,
Guiding souls from day to night.
A realm untouched by sun's warm glow,
Beneath the surface, stories flow.

Crimson tides and cobalt skies,
Where the timid and brave arise.
Veils of blue, a dance so bold,
Lost in whispers, legends told.

In this depth, we find our muse,
A liquid world, a path we choose.
With every breath, we dive anew,
Beneath the surface, life is true.

Tempest's Lullaby

Winds collide with thunder's roar,
Nature's power, fierce, hardcore.
Yet in chaos, beauty sings,
A sweet solace that storm brings.

Clouds like waves in twilight's fight,
Crashing dark, then softening light.
Raindrops fall like a tender kiss,
A dance of nature, pure bliss.

Edged by lightning, shadows play,
In tempest's heart, night turns to day.
Songs of storms wrap hearts so tight,
Tempest's lullaby, pure delight.

Calm follows in the wake so sweet,
With scents of earth beneath our feet.
In the quiet, dreams begin,
The lull of storms, hearts the same twin.

Nature's breath, a rhythmic pulse,
In every storm, a world convulse.
Sing now the song of earth and sky,
In tempest's hush, let spirits fly.

Shimmering Abyss

In the depths where shadows gleam,
Wonders hide like a waking dream.
Light cascades through azure streams,
In the abyss, life softly teems.

Colors swirl in silent night,
Mysteries cloaked from the light.
Echoes drift, a haunting call,
In shimmering depths, we rise and fall.

Glimmers dance on watery skin,
The pull of currents deep within.
A siren's whisper, soft and sweet,
In the abyss, hearts dare to beat.

Jewel-toned schools move as one,
In the silence before the sun.
In harmony, the silence sways,
In shimmering depths, lost in a haze.

Embrace the dark, where secrets lie,
In the abyss, stars fill the sky.
With every glance, a new embrace,
Shimmering depths, a sacred space.

Time Encased

Moments captured, frozen still,
In amber light, we feel the thrill.
Each tick echoes, a timeless song,
Through all the ages, we belong.

Memories weave a tapestry bright,
Woven dreams in day and night.
In each heartbeat, stories unfurl,
In the embrace of a timeless world.

Clock hands dance, a delicate waltz,
In the sphere where past defaults.
Hold on tight, for time can flee,
In memories stitched, we wander free.

Whispers of old still guide our way,
In echoes of those who dared to stay.
Framed in moments, love's sweet trace,
A timeless grace we cannot replace.

As seasons change and years unfold,
In each story, we find the gold.
With every breath, we chase and race,
Time encased in a warm embrace.

The Stilled Flow

In twilight whispers, waters rest,
Beneath the stars, in silence dressed.
A gentle breeze, a breath held tight,
Nature's song fades into night.

Moonlight dances on the skin,
Where shadows dwell, the dreams begin.
Each wave a memory etched in time,
A haunting echo, pure and sublime.

Reflections bend in tranquil grace,
The stillness speaks, a sacred space.
As whispers weave through moments lost,
The stilled flow dreams, no longer tossed.

In ripples soft, a tale unfolds,
Of secret worlds and stories told.
In waters deep, the heart will find,
The quiet peace that soothes the mind.

So linger here by banks so fair,
Feel nature's breath, the cool night air.
Embrace the calm, let worries go,
In the stilled flow, let your heart glow.

Liquid Ice

Upon the lake, a mirror shines,
Captured dreams in crystal lines.
It glimmers bright, a cold display,
Where frozen thoughts begin to play.

With every breath, the silence grows,
As winter's chill in stillness flows.
A fragile edge, where time stands still,
In liquid ice, the world can thrill.

Beneath the surface, secrets sleep,
In frozen depths, the echoes creep.
A realm of silence softly calls,
In liquid ice, where beauty falls.

The sun will rise, the thaw will come,
Yet here we pause, the stillness hums.
In fleeting moments, capture grace,
In liquid ice, find your embrace.

So take a breath, let thought be light,
In this embrace of cold and bright.
As time unfolds with gentle sighs,
In every heart, the liquid lies.

Frosted Echoes

The morning sun paints fields of white,
Frosted echoes in soft daylight.
Whispers of winter, pure and clear,
A world transformed, we hold so dear.

Glistening branches, sparkled dreams,
In every corner, nature beams.
A tapestry of ice and glow,
Frosted echoes, breathes life so slow.

Amidst the stillness, shadows dance,
In frozen beauty, we take our chance.
Each step a sound, a crunch so sweet,
In frosted echoes, hearts gently meet.

As daylight wanes and chill descends,
The frosted whispers softly blend.
We gather close, in warmth we find,
In frosted echoes, love entwined.

So linger here, let moments linger,
In frost and light, let joy be singer.
In every breath, the world ignites,
In frosted echoes, pure delights.

Enchanted Slumber

As twilight drapes the day in blue,
The world retreats, a soft adieu.
In dreams we wander, far and wide,
In enchanted slumber, we take a ride.

Whispers of night, the stars appear,
A lullaby only dreamers hear.
In shimmers soft, our hopes unfold,
In enchanted slumber, stories bold.

Each breath a canvas, colors blend,
In sleep's embrace, all troubles mend.
Through realms of magic, our spirits soar,
In enchanted slumber, forevermore.

Where wishes nestle in midnight air,
And every heartbeat lays us bare.
In twilight's arms, we find our place,
In enchanted slumber, dreams embrace.

So close your eyes, let shadows play,
In peaceful night, drift far away.
In silent whispers, hearts align,
In enchanted slumber, love divine.

The Breath of Winter's Ocean

The ocean breathes a chilly sigh,
Waves wrap the shore in frosted lace.
Underneath the muted sky,
Whispers of winter's cold embrace.

Seagulls glide on silver wings,
Tracing lines in the bitter air.
Each gust a song of frozen things,
Nature's canvas, stark and bare.

Pebbles shimmer, kissed by frost,
Crystals dance beneath the moon.
In this world, nothing's lost,
Every echo tells a tune.

Footprints fade on snowy strands,
Left by wanderers in the night.
The ocean stretches, vast and grand,
Beneath the stars, a blanket white.

As dawn awakens, soft and pale,
The breath of winter starts to fade.
Yet in the waves, a timeless tale,
Of beauty in the cold displayed.

Winter’s Lament Over Silent Waters

Above the lake, a silence falls,
Winter drapes her veils of snow.
The world listens to nature's calls,
As breath of frost begins to grow.

Dark waters hide beneath the sheen,
Reflecting whispers of the grey.
Trees stand tall, a ghostly scene,
While clouds weave dreams that float away.

Each ripple tells of frosty nights,
When stars vanish in the fray.
A distant echo, soft delights,
As shadows dance where children play.

But echoes fade with winter’s breath,
In solitude, the waters weep.
A beauty found in quiet death,
In dreams of summer, still they sleep.

With every breath, the world awaits,
The thaw that marks the end of cold.
But for now, the sorrow states,
That winter’s tale is yet untold.

Glacial Whispers

In silent caves where ice resides,
Whispers echo through the stone.
Secrets kept where beauty hides,
In glacial realms, forever alone.

The light cascades in hues of blue,
Painting walls with nature’s art.
Each crystal glimmers, fresh and new,
In snowflakes’ dance, they play their part.

Beneath the weight of time’s embrace,
Rivers carve their stories deep.
In every curve, a frozen grace,
A language that the mountains keep.

Echoes of the ages past,
Hang in air, both sharp and sweet.
Nature’s history held steadfast,
A rhythmic pulse beneath our feet.

As dusk falls soft on icebound land,
The world shimmers under pale light.
With every breath, we understand,
Glacial whispers, silent night.

Shattered Horizons

Where mountains touch the endless sky,
Horizons break in jagged lines.
The sunset melts, a vibrant dye,
As shadows weave through ancient pines.

In twilight's grasp, the silence hums,
A symphony of fractured light.
Each peak and valley softly thrums,
With tales that whisper through the night.

The breath of dusk, a fleeting chance,
To witness beauty's fragile thread.
Each moment holds a fleeting dance,
As darkness cloaks the day once led.

Stars emerge with glimmers bright,
Chasing shadows into dreams.
The world begins to lose its fight,
In shattered horizons, nothing seems.

Yet in the void, a spark ignites,
Hope flickers softly, warm and clear.
Through shattered skies, the heart ignites,
And finds its way amidst the fear.

Beneath a Shroud of Frost

Beneath a shroud of frost we tread,
Whispers of winter dance in our head.
Silvery blankets, soft and light,
Cradling dreams in the still of night.

Trees wear crystals, gleaming bright,
Stars twinkle softly, pure delight.
Footprints trace the silent ground,
In this frozen world, solace found.

Moonlight spills on icy lakes,
A shimmering path each step it makes.
Cold air cradles our breath in white,
Painting stories of winter's might.

The world in slumber, hushed and deep,
As shadows weave, the night we keep.
In nature's grasp, we find our place,
In the chilling grip, a warm embrace.

Beneath a shroud, our hearts entwine,
Each frosted breath, a fleeting sign.
Together we wander, hand in hand,
In this enchanted, ice-bound land.

Captive Waves of a Polar Night

Captive waves in the polar night,
Whispering secrets, silent plight.
Frozen tides that ebb and flow,
Guarding stories we long to know.

The moon hangs low with a silver sheen,
Painting darkness, a glowing scene.
Stars like diamonds, sharp and clear,
Cast their light, drawing us near.

Frigid winds carry distant songs,
Echoing where the night belongs.
Each pulse of water, deep and wide,
Holds the mysteries of the tide.

In this realm where shadows dance,
We find ourselves in a frozen trance.
Under the sky's vast, twinkling dome,
The waves beckon, calling us home.

Captive waves, forever bold,
Cradle secrets from ages old.
Within their grasp, we dream anew,
In the heart of night, just me and you.

Lullaby of the Frozen Deep

Lullaby of the frozen deep,
Where the icy currents gently sweep.
Cradled in blue, the silence sings,
Of ancient tales and hidden things.

Beneath the surface, secrets lie,
Ghostly shadows, drifting by.
The echoes of life, soft and light,
Dance in the depths of endless night.

Whitecaps shimmer like stars above,
In the cold embrace, I feel your love.
Waves lull us into blissful dreams,
Where the world is nothing as it seems.

Here in the depths, we're never alone,
Each heartbeat pulses, a soothing tone.
Under the ice, we find our peace,
In the hush of the ocean, sweet release.

Lullabies whisper from the sea,
Of journeys taken, wild and free.
Dreams swell and surge with the tide,
In the frozen deep, we abide.

Shattered Reflections on Arctic Waters

Shattered reflections on arctic waters,
A world distorted, nature's daughters.
Glacial shards like fragments of dreams,
Catch the light in splintered beams.

Each ripple tells a story past,
Of seasons gone, of love unsurpassed.
Floating ice like a painter's brush,
Colors melding in a silent hush.

Silhouettes of mountains echo high,
In the mirror's grip, they sway and sigh.
The dance of light, a fleeting show,
In reflections deep, we lose and grow.

Daylight wanes, the sky ablaze,
An artist's palette, a fiery haze.
In the fading glow, we stand in awe,
At the beauty captured in nature's law.

Shattered reflections guide the way,
Through the landscapes where spirits play.
In this realm where waters gleam,
We find our truth, living the dream.

Shimmering Dreams on a Shivering Sea

The waves whisper secrets soft,
As moonlight dances, stars aloft.
Each shimmer holds a tale untold,
Of dreams that shimmer, bright and bold.

In the night, the breezes sigh,
Carrying wishes that drift and fly.
The sea reflects a world unreal,
Where hopes and fears begin to heal.

Beneath the surface, shadows play,
Crafting stories in their sway.
Colors blend, a painter's stroke,
Awakening visions, gently evoked.

As dawn breaks, the night retreats,
Yet in our hearts, the magic beats.
The shimmering dreams still linger near,
A reminder that joy can appear.

With every tide, new dreams arise,
Beneath the vast, all-seeing skies.
Together, we'll sail from shore to shore,
Chasing dreams forevermore.

The Hidden Flow Underneath

Beneath the earth, a river winds,
In secret realms, its path unwinds.
Silent currents tell their tale,
In the dark, where shadows sail.

Whispers echo in the stone,
Stories of the lost and lone.
Drops of water, crystal clear,
Flow through ages, calms our fear.

Roots entwine, a sacred bond,
Bringing life to earth beyond.
Each heartbeat thrums in whispered streams,
Sustaining all of nature's dreams.

The hidden flow, a journey wise,
Where wisdom flows, beneath the skies.
It shapes the land, a gentle hand,
Guiding life in soft command.

In every drop, a mystery,
In every wave, a history.
Let us listen and believe,
In the flow that helps us weave.

Mysteries of the Luminous Ice

The ice glows bright in twilight's hold,
Secrets nestled in the cold.
Crystalline structures weave their light,
Painting stories through the night.

Frozen lakes with whispers low,
Echoing all that we don't know.
Each shimmer tells of time's embrace,
In the stillness, we find grace.

Beneath the surface, shadows creep,
Guarding wishes, dreams we keep.
In the luminous glow of frozen tears,
Lie the echoes of our fears.

The chilly breeze sings soft and low,
Stirring hearts with tales to flow.
Luminous ice, a mirror clear,
Reflecting hopes that draw us near.

As we touch the frost's embrace,
We feel the pulse of ancient space.
In mysteries carved by nature's hand,
We find the beauty in this land.

A Reverie Between the Crags

Nestled high, where mountains meet,
In a cradle, soft and sweet.
Nature's beauty, raw and grand,
Calls to hearts across the land.

Crisp air wraps around my soul,
Filling spaces, making whole.
Whispers float on winds that sway,
Guiding thoughts in rich array.

Crags stand tall, steadfast and proud,
Guardians of the misty shroud.
Through their gaps, the sunlight beams,
Weaving light into our dreams.

Each step echoes in the stone,
Connecting paths we walk alone.
In this haven, time stands still,
Filling hearts with warmth and will.

A reverie, where spirits roam,
Finding solace, feeling home.
Between the crags, we breathe anew,
In this realm, with skies so blue.

The Silent Symphony Beneath

In the hush of winter's embrace,
Nature whispers soft and low,
A melody of frozen grace,
Where silent currents gently flow.

Beneath the ice, secrets reside,
A world unseen and still so grand,
Echoes of life in silence hide,
In nature's quiet, hand in hand.

Footsteps crunch on powdered snow,
Each sound a note in winter's song,
The trees adorned, a frosty show,
In harmony, they dance along.

Stars above in velvet night,
Shimmer like diamonds in the deep,
They cast a glow, a tranquil light,
Where dreams and shadows softly creep.

Together, we embrace the cold,
Wrapped in warmth, our spirits blend,
In this symphony of gold,
Winter's magic will never end.

Glacial Dreams on Waves of White

Upon the shores of crystal dreams,
The waves caress with icy breath,
In glacial hues and silver gleams,
They whisper secrets of sweet death.

Through frosted mists, the visions gleam,
A world adorned in silken frost,
Where every flake, a fragile dream,
On nature's canvas, never lost.

The horizon stretches wide and clear,
A blanket white, pure as the day,
In glacial realms, we find no fear,
But joy amidst the cold ballet.

Reflections dance in frozen light,
Each ripple tells a tale of old,
A symphony of dark and bright,
Where heart and soul reclaim the bold.

So let us wander, hand in hand,
On waves of white, where dreams ignite,
In glacial lands, a timeless strand,
We chase the stars into the night.

Twilight’s Kiss on Frozen Waves

As twilight falls on frozen seas,
The sky ignites with hues of gold,
A gentle breeze, a whispered tease,
In chilly arms, our dreams unfold.

The waves reflect a canvas bright,
With shades that dance and melt away,
In twilight's kiss, the world feels right,
As shadows play on winter’s gray.

Each moment captured, time stands still,
The frozen waves a silent song,
With every pulse, they seem to thrill,
In twilight’s glow, we drift along.

Beneath the stars, we find our way,
In nature's heart, we carve our space,
With every breath, the night will sway,
In frozen waves, we find our grace.

So hold me close as day departs,
In twilight’s arms, our spirits soar,
With every beat, entwined our hearts,
On frozen waves, we seek for more.

Reflections of a Winter's Heart

In winter's breath, the world stands still,
A mirror held to nature's face,
Each flake a whisper, soft and chill,
Reflections dance in time and space.

The trees, a gallery of white,
Stand tall beneath the heavy sky,
Their branches cradle dreams of night,
In silent grace, they watch and sigh.

A frozen stream, a glassy glide,
With stories trapped beneath its skin,
Each ripple holds a tide of pride,
In winter's heart, we find within.

So let us wander through this scene,
Where silence speaks in tones so pure,
In every breath, a hidden sheen,
The winter's heart, forever sure.

Together here, with hands entwined,
We walk through snowflakes, light as air,
In reflections, our souls aligned,
A winter's heart, a love we share.

A Sea Held Hostage by Ice

The waves once danced, a swirling blue,
Now frozen crystal, silent, true.
A captive tide, lost in its plight,
Beneath the cold, there hides a light.

Frostbitten whispers chill the air,
A tale of woe, a frozen snare.
Beneath the shell, the ocean sighs,
As winter's grasp confines the skies.

Ghostly echoes hum their tune,
While shadows lurk beneath the moon.
A boat once sailed, now anchored tight,
In icy talons, stripped of flight.

Yet in the depths, a heart still beats,
A warmth remains where silence greets.
The grip of ice, though strong it seems,
Can never shatter ocean dreams.

So wait for spring, for sun's embrace,
The sea will thaw, reclaim its space.
The ice will melt, the waves return,
And deep within, the tides will churn.

Enchanted By the Whispering Chill

In the grip of frost, secrets dwell,
Whispering chill weaves its spell.
Each flake a note from winter's song,
As silence wraps the world along.

Trees wear crystals, glistening bright,
Branches lace with shards of light.
The winds weave tales of ages past,
In frosty breaths, the shadows cast.

Footsteps crunch on powdered ground,
In the stillness, dreams are found.
A moment held in icy breath,
Where time stands still, as still as death.

Nature hums a lullaby,
Beneath a gray and heavy sky.
In this realm, we pause and feel,
The magic deep, the cool, the real.

So let the chill embrace your soul,
Let winter’s whispers make you whole.
For in this frost, we find our grace,
A tranquil heart in nature's space.

Lanterns of Ice Beneath the Tide

Beneath the waves where dark meets light,
Glows lanterns made of purest white.
They shimmer soft like distant stars,
Guardians of dreams, from near to far.

With every pulse, they rise and fall,
In rhythmic dances, they enthrall.
A world where silence holds its crown,
And icy whispers never drown.

Time drifts like currents on a glide,
As secrets kept in depths abide.
The lanterns flicker with each sway,
A beacon bright in blue decay.

Nautical ghosts that gently guide,
In depths where mysteries reside.
Their light a solace in the dark,
A reminder of the hidden spark.

So dive deep into the endless night,
Where icy lanterns share their light.
Embrace the depths, let passions flow,
In a dance of dreams beneath the glow.

The Shimmering Abyss of Sleep

In twilight's hush, the world will fade,
To realms where dreams and shadows wade.
The shimmering abyss softly calls,
Where time suspends and silence falls.

Each sigh a wave, a thought adrift,
In sleep's embrace, we find our gift.
The stars above in slumber shine,
While thoughts entwine with the divine.

In midnight's depth, our spirits soar,
Past veils of sleep, to distant shore.
A tranquil sea of whispered lore,
Awaits the heart, forevermore.

Lullabies of darkness sway,
Guiding weary minds away.
In gentle arms, we lose the fight,
As night bestows its purest light.

So close your eyes, let dreams take flight,
In the shimmering abyss of night.
For there you'll find what hearts still keep,
A sacred place, a vow to leap.

Congealed Memories

In the attic, shadows creep,
Dusty whispers, secrets keep.
Faded photographs in view,
Time stands still, but not for you.

Moments locked in amber light,
Silent echoes, lost from sight.
Fragments of a life once known,
Carved in stone, yet overthrown.

Tangled dreams and timid sighs,
Haunting echoes, soft goodbyes.
Resonations of the past,
Wishing time would hold them fast.

Glimmers of a joy long gone,
Flickering like a waning dawn.
In this stillness, hearts may mend,
Congealed memories, never end.

Glacial Tidepool

In the cradle of the ice,
Life teems in water’s splice.
Creatures dance on frozen floor,
Secrets held in tidal lore.

Beneath the surface, colors gleam,
Echoes of a watery dream.
Resilient hearts, they sway and weave,
In the calm, they find reprieve.

Whispers swirl through icy air,
Nature’s art, beyond compare.
Harmony in stillness found,
In glacial tide, life is profound.

Fingers of the water spread,
Where the light and shadows tread.
In the stillness, beauty calls,
Glacial tidepool, where life enthralls.

Shimmering Stillness

Beneath the moon's soft silver glow,
The world in quiet beauty flows.
A tranquil lake, a mirror wide,
Reflects the stars, the night's sweet pride.

Gentle ripples kiss the shore,
Whispers of the night restore.
Silhouette of dreams at play,
In shimmering stillness, night turns day.

Nature breathes, a soft embrace,
Calm descends in this sacred space.
Time drifts slow, each moment clear,
In shimmering stillness, we draw near.

Leaves rustle softly in the breeze,
Echoes linger, hearts at ease.
Within this world, peace intertwines,
Shimmering stillness, love defines.

Brittle Waters

In winter’s clutch, the world turns gray,
Brittle waters, fading away.
Reflections fracture in the frost,
Silent whispers of what’s lost.

Crystalline forms on edges cling,
Nature's beauty, a fragile thing.
Ice-bound realms where dreams may freeze,
Capturing moments, hearts to tease.

Rivers slacken, slow their flow,
Each drop holds tales we cannot know.
Yet in their depths, a story cries,
Brittle waters, truth never lies.

Breaking surfaces with a sigh,
The heart of water seeks to fly.
In soft decay, there lies rebirth,
Brittle waters, a tale of worth.

Icy Embrace

Cold winds whisper through the trees,
Branches heavy, some to seize.
A blanket white enfolds the ground,
In winter's grip, silence is found.

Glistening jewels on frozen leaves,
Nature pauses, time believes.
Hearts entwined in a chill so deep,
In icy embrace, secrets we keep.

Footsteps crunch on snow so bright,
In the stillness, a shared light.
The world breathes softly, dreams take flight,
Under the stars, all feels right.

Frosted breath on a moonlit night,
The chill invites, the warmth ignites.
Holding close in the frosty air,
In this moment, we lay bare.

Winter whispers, love's refrain,
In icy embrace, joy and pain.
The heart beats softly, echoes sound,
In frozen wonder, we are found.

Beneath the Frost

Under layers of delicate ice,
Whispers of life, hidden, precise.
The world below, still and profound,
Beneath the frost, secrets abound.

Silent stories softly told,
Of days gone by, of dreams bold.
Nature sleeps in stillness tight,
Wrapped in blankets of pure white.

Glimmers faint, like stars on ground,
Hope and warmth waiting to be found.
Each breath held, time slows its race,
A tranquil heart in winter's grace.

Gentle thaws as the sun will rise,
Kisses of warmth from azure skies.
From silent depths to vibrant bloom,
Beneath the frost, life will resume.

Awakening whispers, nature's call,
Emerging moments, ready to all.
As daylight breaks, the past unfurls,
Beneath the frost, a new world swirls.

Crystal Currents

Rivers run with crystal souls,
Flowing freely, the current rolls.
Beneath the surface, stories weave,
In the depths, our hearts believe.

Reflecting skies of azure bright,
Dancing sparkles in morning light.
The water hums a soothing tune,
Carrying whispers 'neath the moon.

Life awakens in gentle streams,
Where nature nurtures all our dreams.
Swiftly moving, the currents twist,
In every ripple, memories kissed.

Branches dip, leaves intertwined,
In crystal currents, peace we find.
The journey far, yet close at hand,
Flowing onward, in life we stand.

Lost in motion, a tranquil dance,
Each wave brings forth a second chance.
As waters part, new paths reveal,
In crystal currents, hearts can heal.

Abandoned Shores

Where the waves meet sand so bare,
Whispers echo, memories share.
Abandoned shores, a tale untold,
Of secrets kept and dreams of old.

Driftwood scattered, time's embrace,
Nature's art in a silent space.
Footprints fading with the tide,
Treasures lost, but hearts abide.

Seagulls cry in the open air,
Their calls linger, a breath of care.
The ocean breathes, vast and wide,
In countless stories, we confide.

Waves crashing in a soothing song,
In the stillness, we belong.
Abandoned shores, yet filled with light,
Guiding souls through the darkest night.

As the sun dips, colors blend,
Each moment cherished with time to spend.
Abandoned, yet alive once more,
In every heartbeat on the shore.

Echoes of Winter

Silent whispers in the night,
Frosted breath and pale moonlight.
Bare branches sway with a sigh,
As winter's chill begins to fly.

Footsteps crunch on the frozen ground,
Nature's lullaby, a soft sound.
A blanket white, so pure, so bright,
Echoes linger in the still night.

Snowflakes dance in the frigid air,
Carpeting earth with gentle care.
Every flake a memory spun,
In winter's grasp, we become one.

Clouds drift slowly, heavy and gray,
Marking the end of another day.
The world transformed, a pristine sight,
Bathed in silence, draped in white.

In the warmth of a fire's glow,
We find comfort, soft and slow.
As the frost bites at the pane,
Winter's magic, sweet refrain.

Submerged Silence

Beneath the ice, the world sleeps still,
Wrapped in quiet, a winter chill.
Voices muffled, time stands tall,
In this moment, we hear the call.

Waves of stillness, currents freeze,
Nature pauses, a gentle tease.
Thoughts submerged within the deep,
Resting softly, layered in sleep.

Crystals shimmer, a hidden shine,
Secrets dwell in the cold divine.
Every breath, a frozen sigh,
In the vastness, whispers lie.

Branches bowed with heavy weight,
Echoes gather, whispering fate.
Darkness wraps the earth around,
In this silence, peace is found.

A world submerged, holding its breath,
In the stillness, life and death.
Time stretches, a quiet trance,
In winter's hold, we pause and dance.

Fragments of Ice

Splintered shards on a frozen lake,
Reflecting dreams, a slight mistake.
Each piece holds a story true,
In fragments found, reflections new.

Melting moments whisper low,
Echoes of soft laughter flow.
Underneath the chilly skin,
Life awakens, begins again.

Glimmers catch the morning sun,
A dazzling show has just begun.
Each fragment shines with memories bright,
Illuminated in the light.

Rippling echoes of days gone past,
In these pieces, shadows cast.
Every edge, a tale untold,
In silence, beauty unfolds.

As winter wanes, the ice will melt,
But in our hearts, the fragments felt.
Though transient, they leave their mark,
In the quiet, they spark a spark.

Winter's Grasp

Clenched in winter's icy hold,
The world wrapped in a tale of old.
Barren fields stretch out in white,
Underneath the cover of night.

Frost on windows, breath turns to steam,
In this season, we softly dream.
Each moment lingers, time stands still,
In winter's grasp, the heart can fill.

Chill winds dance through the trees,
Whispering secrets with elegant ease.
Snowflakes twirl in the gentle breeze,
As nature bows with graceful pleas.

Warmth of hearth against the chill,
Echoes of laughter, time to fill.
The world outside may freeze and sting,
But within, the heart finds spring.

So let us gather, hold close, unite,
As winter weaves its cloak of white.
In every flake, a magic cast,
In winter's beauty, we find our vast.

Lassitude of the Arctic Tides

The waves sigh soft, a gentle fade,
Beneath the moon's pale silver blade.
A chilly breeze whispers low,
In tranquil dance, the tides do flow.

Pale glaciers drift on azure seas,
While stars twinkle in the evening breeze.
Their light reflects on waters bright,
As darkness swallows the fading light.

Lonely shores where silence weaves,
In frosty breaths, the spirit grieves.
A world entwined in icy grasp,
Where fleeting moments gently clasp.

Beneath the stillness, secrets lie,
In depths where ancient echoes sigh.
The Arctic's heart beats slow and deep,
In dreams of ice, the waters sleep.

A canvas wrapped in white embrace,
The tides flow softly, time, a trace.
In lassitude, the night concedes,
To whispers of the frozen reeds.

Echoes of Ice in the Night

In the still dark, the shadows gleam,
Ice crystals catch the moon's silver beam.
Silent whispers drift through the air,
As the world holds its breath in despair.

Glacial echoes break the deep,
Songs from the cold, where secrets seep.
The night wraps tight with a shimmering veil,
In frozen dreams where spirits sail.

Stars like diamonds in the sky glow bright,
As frost-kissed winds carry the night.
Each breath of chill tells stories untold,
In frozen realms where time is old.

Mysterious shadows dance along the shore,
In the echoes of ice, we yearn for more.
A haunting lullaby teems with grace,
In the heart of the night, a sacred place.

The world lies wrapped in a tranquil peace,
As whispers of ice never cease.
With every breath, the echoes abide,
In the stillness where secrets reside.

The Stillness Holds the Secrets

Silent whispers float through the air,
Stillness lingers, secrets laid bare.
The frozen land, a canvas clear,
Reveals the truths we seldom hear.

In crisp white snow, footsteps make trails,
Carrying tales in hushed exhale.
Each breath released, a fleeting sound,
In the stillness, what have we found?

Beneath the surface, a heartbeat hums,
The pulse of nature, a rhythm comes.
In quiet realms, the world will keep,
The ancient stories, buried deep.

Horizon meets the icy glow,
Where colors merge and stillness flows.
In frozen embrace, the dusk ignites,
A canvas of dreams under night lights.

As silence reigns in purest form,
And winter's breath begins to warm.
The stillness holds all we seek,
In the tranquil heart, we hear it speak.

Whispers in a Sea of Ivory

Upon the waves, a hush prevails,
A sea of ivory gently entails.
The whispers rise like soft-spun threads,
Carried by winds where silence spreads.

Each crest a canvas, stark and clear,
Hides tales of sorrow, joy, and cheer.
In the frosty air, the echoes soar,
With every splash, they ask for more.

The pale horizon meets the deep blue,
Where dreams are born and moments brew.
In ivory swells, a serene embrace,
The ocean shares its secret space.

Beneath the surface, shadows glide,
In swirling depths where memories hide.
With gentle nudges, the tides recite,
The whispered vows of day and night.

In the tapestry of frost and foam,
Whispers linger, calling us home.
In a sea where ivory meets the sky,
The timeless tales of the deep sigh.

Chilled Reflections

In the mirror of ice, shadows gleam,
Whispers of frost in a silvery dream.
Silent echoes dance in the night,
Chilled reflections bathed in pale light.

Snowflakes twirl, a soft ballet,
Nature's canvas in shades of gray.
Breath of winter, crisp and clear,
Hushed murmurs only the heart can hear.

Moonlight casts its tender glow,
Painting the world in a tranquil flow.
Each flake a story, a gentle sigh,
As the night serenades the sky.

Time stands still in this frozen land,
Nature's beauty at every hand.
With each heartbeat, the silence swells,
In chilled reflections, the spirit dwells.

The Still Depths

Beneath the surface, secrets lie,
Waves of whispers, soft and shy.
Echoes woven in calm despair,
In the still depths, we breathe the air.

Cool currents cradle thoughts so deep,
Where ancient shadows gently creep.
Mysteries float on dreamlike tides,
In the still depths, the heart abides.

Glimmers of light stir the dark,
Fleeting visions, a silent spark.
With every pulse, the silence grows,
In the still depths, serenity flows.

Time slips softly, a muted stream,
Weaving the fabric of a quiet dream.
Where stillness reigns, and thoughts take flight,
In the still depths, is endless night.

Hyperborean Dreams

In the land where the sun takes a pause,
Beneath the glow of the Northern stars.
Whispers of ancient, untouched grace,
Hyperborean dreams in a timeless space.

Frost-tinged air holds tales untold,
Of glacial giants and treasures bold.
Dancing lights in a mystical swirl,
Within these dreams, the wonders unfurl.

In a kingdom where winter weaves,
A fabric fine that no heart leaves.
Crystals whisper from heights so steep,
Hyperborean dreams drift into sleep.

Each breath laced with magic’s essence,
Boundless moments, time’s presence.
Awake in this chill, yet warm embrace,
Hyperborean dreams, a wild chase.

Glimmers on the Arctic

Glimmers dance along the ice,
In the Arctic, a world so nice.
Stars descend to kiss the ground,
In the silence, beauty found.

Shadows stretch beneath the glow,
Whispers of the winds that blow.
Every heartbeat sings a tune,
Beneath the watchful winter moon.

Frosted breath in the starlit air,
Moments linger, precious and rare.
In the stillness, dreams ignite,
Glimmers on the Arctic, pure delight.

Nature’s magic, a frozen art,
Awakens stillness within the heart.
With every shimmer, hope does rise,
Glimmers on the Arctic, endless skies.

Echoes in the Deep

Whispers dance in the midnight tide,
Secrets of the ocean, side by side.
Ripples tell tales of long-lost dreams,
Echoes linger in soft moonbeams.

Voices rise from the depths so blue,
Singing songs of the old and new.
In the depths where shadows creep,
Life unfolds in silence deep.

Currents cradle stories untold,
Adventures in waters brave and bold.
Each wave a memory, lost yet found,
In the sea's embrace, mysteries abound.

Stars reflect on the ocean's face,
Guiding sailors on their race.
Tides of time in rhythm sway,
Leading hearts where dreams can play.

Underneath where sunbeams fail,
Twilight mingles with the pale.
Echoes rise from the ocean's floor,
Calling to those who seek for more.

Enigmas of the Cold

Snowflakes fall like whispered lies,
Falling softly from clouded skies.
Each one unique, a fleeting glance,
Enigmas wrapped in winter's dance.

Frosty breath hangs in the air,
Framing trees with delicate care.
Nature's canvas, pure and white,
Painting the world in cold delight.

Icicles glisten, sharp as dreams,
Underneath the pale sunbeams.
Silent whispers through the night,
Echoing secrets, pure and bright.

Beneath the surface, life still stirs,
In the cold, where wonder occurs.
Frozen ponds with stories to share,
Guarding treasures hidden with care.

In this realm of chilling grace,
Every moment holds a trace.
Of warmth and laughter, of fireside glow,
A reminder of life beneath the snow.

Fluctuating Frost

Morning light glimmers on the glass,
A dance of frost as moments pass.
Patterns twist, a delicate show,
Kissed by sunlight, they ebb and flow.

Each breath taken, a cloud appears,
Whispers of winter, laced with cheers.
Nature spins tales in frozen threads,
Awakening dreams from chilly beds.

Glistening landscapes, paintings unfold,
Every corner, a sight to behold.
Fluctuating warmth, then the chill,
Moments fleeting, time to distill.

Rippling echoes in the frosted air,
Reminders of joy, earthy and rare.
Chasing shadows, lost in mirth,
Crystals reflect the beauty of earth.

As evening falls, the soft glow fades,
Leaves a whisper in twilight shades.
Frost retreats under the moon's watch,
While dreams awaken, hearts to clutch.

Silence Beneath

In the hush of night, feelings dwell,
Secrets held in a silent shell.
Stars twinkle, but stillness reigns,
In whispers soft, the heart explains.

Gentle shadows move and sway,
Secrets of the night at play.
The world outside has come to rest,
While thoughts reside in quiet zest.

Beneath the surface, murmurs flow,
Silence hides what we may know.
In the stillness, truths emerge,
As dreams and thoughts begin to surge.

An echoing heart, a restful mind,
In the layers where solace we find.
Silent prayers and wishes keep,
In the cradle of night, we softly creep.

When dawn arrives to claim the day,
Silence wraps dreams, urging them to stay.
In the morning's light, we'll carry on,
The echoes of silence, a soothing song.

Secrets in Ice

Whispers in the frozen air,
Stories buried, secrets rare.
Crystal shards holding light,
Glimmer softly, pure and white.

Beneath the surface, shadows hide,
Frozen tears, a river of pride.
Nature's breath, a silent plea,
In this world, just you and me.

Every crack a tale untold,
A silent witness, wise and old.
Moments captured, held so tight,
In the stillness of the night.

From the mountains to the sea,
Frozen realms of mystery.
In the depths, we find our way,
Guided by the light of day.

Veils of white, where dreams reside,
In their beauty, we confide.
Secrets linger, clear as glass,
In the ice, time cannot pass.

Ethereal Currents

Underneath a shimmering sky,
Flowing softly, dreams pass by.
Water dances, bold and free,
Ethereal waves, a mystery.

Every ripple tells a tale,
Carried gently on the gale.
Nature's brush paints with grace,
In the current's swift embrace.

Silver whispers, secrets shared,
In the depths, hearts are bared.
Navigating through the night,
Guided by the moon’s soft light.

In the shadows, spirits play,
Lost in visions, drift away.
Caught in currents, wild and deep,
In their arms, we find our sleep.

Ethereal dreams, softly flow,
Where the ancient waters go.
Onward, forward, never cease,
In the currents, find your peace.

The Silent Cascade

Glistening rocks, the water spills,
In the hush, the spirit thrills.
Among the trees, a soft embrace,
Nature's heart, a sacred place.

Whispers of a tranquil stream,
Flowing gently, like a dream.
Each droplet carries a sigh,
In the stillness, time slips by.

A cascade sings in quiet tones,
Softly echoing ancient groans.
Lost in wonder, paths unwind,
In the silence, peace we find.

Misty veils of silver fog,
Dancing lightly on the bog.
Gentle currents trace the land,
A soothing touch, a guiding hand.

Nature’s pulse, forever flows,
In the cascade, love bestows.
With every turn, we’re drawn to see,
The silent magic, wild and free.

Frostbitten Waves

Beneath the ice, the ocean sighs,
Whispers lost in frosted tries.
Waves that crash and softly break,
In the cold, the world will wake.

Crystal crests and azure shades,
Nature breathes as sunlight fades.
Frostbitten hands that shape the night,
Guiding stars with gentle light.

Each wave a tale from far away,
Echoes from a distant day.
Rolling forth with ancient grace,
Etched in time, a wondrous space.

Frozen shores and silent sands,
Nature's art made by unseen hands.
In the chill, the spirit roams,
Finding warmth in ocean's homes.

Frostbitten waves, a lullaby,
Where the dreams and waters lie.
In their arms, we learn to play,
Riding on till break of day.

Dreams Bound in Ice

In the stillness, dreams await,
Chained by frost, they hesitate.
A silent world of crystal air,
Frozen hopes linger with despair.

Figures dance in icy glow,
Memories trapped beneath the snow.
Echoes whisper on the breeze,
Lost in time, a heart's unease.

Glimmers of a sunlit past,
A longing held, but never cast.
In this realm, the heart must thaw,
As dreams breathe life, a hopeful law.

Ice-bound wishes, clear yet gray,
Fleeting moments drift away.
Yet in the cold, a fire burns bright,
Guiding dreams through endless night.

Though frozen paths may hold you back,
With every step, you find a track.
Dreams can melt, like morning dew,
Revealing skies of endless blue.

Veil of Snow

A gentle blanket, pure and white,
Enfolding earth in quiet night.
Whispers of wind weave tales untold,
In the silence, secrets unfold.

Snowflakes dance from heavens high,
Each one unique, a fleeting sigh.
Nature's canvas, fresh and clean,
A moment's peace, a tranquil scene.

Beneath the veil, a world sleeps tight,
Held in dreams of soft starlight.
Crystals sparkle, a gem-like gleam,
Awakening hearts, igniting dreams.

Footsteps muffled, echoes soft,
In stillness, spirits lift aloft.
Veil of snow, a tender touch,
Reminding us, we need so much.

As dawn breaks through the silver hues,
Life awakens, all anew.
With every flake, a promise made,
In the embrace of winter's shade.

Celestial Chill

Stars adorn the winter sky,
A celestial chill whispers why.
Moonlight paints the world serene,
A cosmic dance, forever seen.

Galaxies spin in vibrant hues,
Twinkling lights, a cosmic muse.
In the silence, a heartbeat found,
Echoing soft, a wondrous sound.

Frosted beams on flowing streams,
Reflecting all our wildest dreams.
Beneath the chill, deep warmth resides,
In every pulse, the universe bides.

Celestial winds breathe their song,
Bringing forth where souls belong.
In the night, we find our place,
Lost in wonder, a cosmic embrace.

As dawn breaks, the chill retreats,
Yet in heart, its magic beats.
Under the sky, both vast and bright,
We dance in dreams, through day and night.

Whispers of the Abyss

Beneath the waves, a murmur calls,
Whispers hidden in ocean halls.
Darkness shrouds a world below,
Mysteries deep, where shadows flow.

Voices drift in salty air,
Echoes of secrets, a ghostly stare.
In the silence, tales are spun,
Of journeys lost and battles won.

The abyss holds treasures untold,
In depths where time unfolds.
A rhythm beats in waters deep,
Guarding dreams the sea must keep.

As currents swirl, the heart must brave,
Facing fears, the soul to save.
Whispers twist in the watery night,
Guiding lost ships to the light.

So let the waves embrace your soul,
In the abyss, we become whole.
For every whisper, a story lies,
In depths of darkness, the spirit flies.

The Icebound Surface of Echoes

Silent whispers coat the night,
Wrapped in frost, a ghostly sight.
Memories drift on frozen streams,
Echoes linger like distant dreams.

Shadows dance on a pale glow,
Underneath the weight of snow.
Footsteps fade on glistening white,
Lost to the silence, out of sight.

Time stands still, a breath held tight,
In a world draped in icy light.
Voices trapped in winter's hold,
Stories woven, quietly told.

Stars above sparkle cold and bright,
Guiding the way through the deep night.
Every glance reveals the past,
In the silence, shadows cast.

A fragile web of frost is spun,
Beneath the moon, where dreams are run.
The icebound surface speaks so clear,
Of all the things that we hold dear.

Beneath the Frosted Surface

Underneath the snow's soft kiss,
Life stirs in secret, subtle bliss.
Roots entangle in the frozen ground,
Whispers of warmth can still be found.

Layers thick with winter's breath,
Guard the secrets of life and death.
Bubbles trapped in icy glaze,
Hold the stories of brighter days.

The earth sleeps deep in its cocoon,
Awaiting the touch of thawing moon.
Nature's heartbeat, slow and sound,
Beneath the frost, hope is found.

In silence lies the promise bold,
As the thaw takes back the cold.
A world reborn beneath the chill,
Awakens with the springtime will.

Each moment pass, a fleeting chance,
For life to rise in a radiant dance.
Beneath the frost, the pulse won’t cease,
As nature breathes, inviting peace.

Songs of the Winter's Cry

Hollow winds carry their song,
The winter cries, sweet and strong.
Chilling notes fill the frozen air,
Echoes of joy mingled with despair.

Flakes that swirl in a mad ballet,
Singing of night and the fleeting day.
Each gust brings a tale of woe,
Songs of love lost in the snow.

Branches crack under weighty dreams,
Softly falling, or so it seems.
Whispering secrets to the dark,
As shadows glide, leaving a mark.

Ice-coated paths where silence grows,
Footsteps fade as the cold wind blows.
In frosty realms, the heart will sing,
Of winter's wonders—darkness takes wing.

As the world slumbers under the night,
Songs of the winter's cry take flight.
Carried on breezes, they inspire,
A haunting melody of winter's fire.

The Glassy Veil of Forgotten Depths

A surface smooth, like polished glass,
Hides the depths where memories pass.
Veils of time obscure the view,
Of what lies beneath, old yet new.

Reflections dance, a fractured scene,
Of dreams that linger, softly keen.
Silent currents shift and glide,
Buried secrets they can't hide.

Footsteps echo in the stillness,
Tales of longing, sharp with coolness.
The veil between now and then,
Waves of the past, a flowing pen.

In the depths, shadows intertwine,
Threads of stories, yours and mine.
A glassy surface, calm and deep,
Holds the echoes we must keep.

Through the veil, whispers call us near,
To the frozen depths, voice sincere.
As we gaze into the cold embrace,
The past and present interlace.

Milton Keynes UK
Ingram Content Group UK Ltd.
UKHW010233111224
452348UK00011B/716

9 789916 798560